This poetry collection is dedicated to my dear Nigel!

I've taken quite a 'rupi kaur'-esque approach to poetry this time round, but I'm hoping that regardless of such new style and prose, my writing can still excite you!

I hope you're doing well, I miss you so much and can't wait until we reconnect again! Cambridge is only a train away, but my dissertation is more than days away - sadly not enough days to give me the ability to travel elsewhere!

Have a good read!

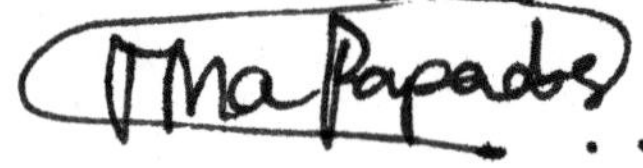

Tina Papados

PACHAMAMA PEACHES
Poetry Collection

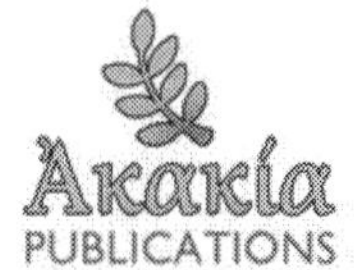

Published in England by AKAKIA Publications, 2017

TINA PAPADOS

PACHAMAMA PEACHES
Poetry Collection

ISBN: 978-1-912322-30-5

Cover Image:
Mixed and Designed by AKAKIA Publications

19 Ashmead, Chase Road,
N14 4QX, London, UK

T. 0044 207 1244 057
F. 0044 203 4325 030

www.akakia.net
publications@akakia.net

2017, London, UK

Pachamama Peaches is a
poetry collection
about
beauty
womanhood
humanity
relationships
art
healing
and nature
all combined together
each poem
serves a separate story
deals with different ideas
provides a particular purpose
Pachamama Peaches takes aspiring readers
to a world of their own
where they can find themselves
within these pages
and begin
to paint their own canvass.

She looked like
a hooker
but spoke like a gentle-
man
she became the whiskey
to my teacup.

Only cinema and war
change all things.

His eyes
were darker than wine,
like a flame of fire.

Our mouths
carry stories
that our hearts
are too afraid
to confess.

To be
Speechless
is to reveal
the loudest roar.

Women are taught
to hate every inch
of their own bodies
all the beauty
that belongs to you
is unappreciated,
shattered
across your beautiful
flesh.

You learn so much
about a person
once they escape from
your mental illness.

His wrinkles
will crawl around his eyes
when he smiles
I'll follow the sun
wherever it takes me
he'll always be there
waiting.

That evening of
drinking red mulled wine
just with you.

He doesn't complete me.
Nor do I
complete him
but,
TO
GET
HER
we create a new world.

The way we dress
can say so much
about our culture
even when
we say so little
ourselves.

Tears of blood
trickling down
your inner thighs
how painful it is
to be a woman.

My love for you
became the last leaf
of a dying tree
quivering from
your untouched love.

I'm celibate, he whispers
after those long years
of being
trapped in cages

My body
is a garden
filled with spikes
for you to prick
your bloody fingers
before you kiss
my velvet rose

His curly locks
resembled the sun
reflected through
the dark waves
of the sea
at breaking dawn.

He's very French
as in
I am mesmerized
at finding it hard
to understand

You can say so much
by revealing so little.

Don't confuse madness
with passion
you'll teach her that
she'll have to suffer
to find love.

It was love at first
conversation
his voice sparked
an intense pleasure
to my mind.

If you love her,
let me know.

I kissed his lips
they were shivering, cold
from all the suffering
you caused him.

I won't trim
the leaves on my legs
just for one night
with you.
I'm searching for a gardener
who appreciates my flowers
and allows me
to grow.

Actors, we are trapped
with skin that never felt at home,
 so we carve it into art.
Carved skin,
out of the soles beneath our shoes
us actors keep on running.

- *Deadly Seven*

I want you
to paint my canvass.

He touches me, and
it feels like the greatest movie
rolling,
it captures our movements
forever.

You don't need a man
to water your interior rose
that's what you have a garden for.

I am mindful
of your silence
it even makes me
want to get a taste
of your thoughts.

My lilies
are not for you to touch
they are not a decoration
a mere plant to water
or a gift for
the death of my love for you.

She had a graspy voice
quite husky and bruised
she resembled a French woman
but spoke like a Russian man
one that never felt at home.

My rouge joined your bruised lips
and in that way
they found their way back home

You'll glare at my ink
and wonder
what it all means
painters don't reveal
the secrets
of each masterpiece.

We all meet for a reason.
you enter a particular train
share glances with strangers
ones you were meant to
exchange visions with
and never see again.

It felt like a thousand bee stings
 even with
 no more honey
to pursue.

As I water my plants
I'll sing to them
 and they'll enjoy it
helps them grow.

I carry my father's sad eyes
 and my mother's warm lips
on my face
they're still together.

His hair was made of
a million sunflowers
bathed in vintage music.

But how
will our emotions ever leave
 us
when they're
painted in acrylic
on this canvass.
It never felt like lust
just *fire*

You can have fun at my festival
just as long as
you remember
to bring the music

You don't want to nourish yourself
with my bruised apple.

- When in the Garden of Eden

There are so many fresh peaches
 to choose from
and yet you choose
 to cut mine.

What is your dream? He asks
not the subconscious desires
but the ones
that keep you up at night.

He smirked at me
whilst his wrinkles supported his eyes,
the windows to his soul.
Those wrinkles
developed wings of their own.

His words
 aroused my mind
producing chemicals
not even love potions would know of.

People will throw knives at you
but you have the power
to protect your canvass.

He watches her closely,
like a camera lens
recording her movements forever.

You can't keep my rose
if you find it grotesque
to have prickled crimson fingers
after violating my thorns.

Women will reach for a rose
prickle their fingers
and apply it like lipstick.
Au Natural.

- *Faut souffrir pour être belle*

You'll share your bodies with strangers
but you won't even share your
toothbrush.

Her golden locks
and navy blue eyes
may excite you
but I am the midnight sky
the dark waves of the sea
flow across my neck
my burgundy eyes
may frighten you
but I am bathed
in rock 'n' roll
and I know
you secretly
love it.

There's so much more to me
than my name
 my eyes
my hair
my face
how can you interpret me
through features I have not chosen
for myself?
Your piercing blue eyes
 make me want to
paint in color
I planted these leaves
 and I will nourish them
so they can grow
to love themselves.

How am I supposed to look
like the women in the magazines
when they themselves
don't look like the women in the magazines?

You taste like rock ‘n’ roll
just like the music
I used to sing.

I wanted him to know
I loved his paintings
but Van Gogh
had his ears cut off.

You're just like a cigarette
People will light you *up*
so they can burn you *down*.

I don't have to explain
the reasons for my body art
you don't ever hear novelists explain
the reasons for their writing.
Yes, I'll paint my women nude
and no, it's not always about sex.
Sex is not bad,
Nudity is not bad,
and you don't have to
always establish
a connection between nudity and sex.

Most men are afraid of what they want.
That's why they'll never get
what they want.

You'll be with a man your whole life
just because he was the first love
you met at seventeen.

You can't have a rose
if you can't handle its thorns.

Your breath tastes like whiskey
the Scottish kind,
the kind I like.

we are taught that
when our thorns produce blood
we become grotesque
to mankind
we should keep to ourselves
and reveal nothing more
than our rose.
we warn women
 to keep their legs shut
 and yet with men
we teach the exact opposite.

Spread your legs
like a canvass
so I can paint you
in acrylic motion.

If a man and a woman
do not appreciate the same films
they will eventually
divorce.

I knew you'd admire
my maple leaves
after all
you are Canadian.

You mention women's periods
as if we're producing bombs
murdering unfertilized children.

Bruises
running down her thighs
words
firing through her mind
she's ecstatic

Did you ever love her?
perhaps
you did

I'll plant wild flowers
in my hair
and follow the sun
wherever it takes me
I'll be free
from you

Let's open up a beer
and have some
sweet champagne
under the sun

Avec Joan à la Seine (2014)

we never said goodbye
perhaps it wasn't
the end
of you and I

She looked like a prostitute
it wasn't a bad thing
I just thought her makeup looked good.

Yes, I carry guns
under my thighs
who knows
when I'll need to

You had no words
and neither did I
we both knew
what was running
through our minds

- You should have kissed me

It's not going to be easy
nobody said
it ever would be
but it won't kill me
to wonder

I was distorted from reality
I wasn't insane
I wasn't strange
you chose to leave because you didn't
love me.

Every passenger you'll meet
on the train
has their own soundtrack
every memory,
every moment,
has a different song playing
for a different human.

That's why we'll never agree
on the perfect soundtrack
for each film

I spent years
growing these leaves
I won't remove them
for a man
who doesn't appreciate my wild garden

You always had a thing
for the younger kind
I know men like you
I've been searching for my father
for a lifetime.

Will you become
my first wife?

Don't disturb the trees
if you're unwilling to
eat a bruised pear.

There's plenty of bananas
on trees
your issue is that
you prefer apples.

Being a hooker
by sleeping with lots of men
doesn't seem so bad if they're cute
I'm pretty sure
    that's just called dating

I don't drink to forget
why would I?
rarely do you get
to meet a woman
like this

- in a bar

I was dancing with myself
and everyone thought
I was mad
they couldn't understand
not when you're immune to the music

I wear dark lipstick
because I choose to
I don't do it for you
I don't need to seduce you

Everyone has cherries on their chests
I'm unsure as to why
 I have to hide mine
do they really upset men so much?

You're wondering
whether you should
cut the apple
after all
I gave you the knife.

If you love two people
go for the second option
 had you truly loved the first
you wouldn't have

fallen

for the second

If you want to cheat
that's fine
do it without me
hearing you

What's so special about full moons anyway?
After all,
we're always alone in soul.

Some women
choose to have children
but I have a dragon
in my womb
because I'd rather
give birth to my art

I want 'The Rachel' haircut.
Can I get a Ross with that?

surya namaskara
breathe in, *exhale*

My name must taste so sweet
it always follows after
those sour words
inside that bitch's mouth.

I am not your second option
I am a peach
for you to eat
or leave
for someone else to feast on.

It wasn't bad of you
to cheat on me with a man
it was bad of you
to think that
you could come back
and be forgiven
because you're just a woman

- *bisexuality has no limits*

How can I love again
when you stole my heart
and took it with you?

His voice
puts me to sleep
but it can also
keep me going for days

You know what I love the most?
People's voices
it's the only thing
which reveals their insides
their thoughts, their minds
are reflected
through conversation
you finally get in touch
with someone's insides
- You're outside, in

If I could live in New York City
I'd have bagels every morning
there's something so exquisite
of beginning your days
as Audrey Hepburn.

The Parisienne had croissants
for breakfast
but she chain-smokes
throughout the day
to make up for it.

If I could put on my Burberry trench coat
 and wear absolutely nothing
underneath
I'd live in paradise.

I have messy waves
I'm young
I'll straighten my hair as I get older
after all
my face will get messier with age

it's all about balance

You'll always find a good reason
to be sitting alone on a bench
read the newspaper
feed the birds
drink your cup of coffee
let them 'people watch' you.

If a woman wants you
trust her instincts
she'll come and find you.

He'll smoke in the cold, outside
to keep himself warm.

Go buy yourself new lingerie
He'll think you have a new lover.

Be soft-spoken
that way,
they'll lean in closer
to hear you.

I actually forget to wear bras
in the summer time.

Maybe I don't go out much.
Perhaps my make-up is too minimal.
In fact, I don't think I even have
The right breasts.
But I do carry a newspaper under my arm
I might mention Rousseau
or Locke in conversation.
It's my mind that' sexually empowering
and that frightens people.

- The Parisian woman

You'll get offended
if I wear too much black.
I didn't mean to
dress for your misery
or funeral.

Toes sink into the sand
you realize you're stepping on foreign soil
but you love the sound
of these calm waves
singing along the midnight sea
there's nothing quite like it

You should come over
listen to my vinyl records
I create my own soundtrack
perhaps
that'll give you more time
to decide
if you want to
ever dance with me.

He shaved
his legs
and they looked great
everyone knew
he looked better than most
women

At the end of a shower
spray your breasts
with cold water

- *you'll thank me later*

We are equal
it is just
our fruits
which part us

I'd rather spend the evenings
with Dali and Lempicka
at least they'd be willing to
inspire my canvass

There will be moments in life
that will feel like the end of time
but it won't be
you just wait

Only can a movie
transport your mind
to a different place

- take me away, Quentin

Women fear to be alone.
But only then are they capable of love.
To love the deepest core of a man
without possessing his trees,
without being dependent on his branches
without reducing a man to paper,
without becoming addicted
to his maple leaves

Paintings of nude women
don't have to be erotic

- I'm upset if that's all you can see

Erotic films are not filth
when they serve an artistic cause
it is those who lack
an artistic drive
that are filthy.

To keep a relationship, whether a partner
or a friend
the ultimate bond is conversation.

Cut up a peach
grow a lily
let a blackbird spread its wings
even nature reveals the flair of a woman.

Your words
consumed my thoughts
suddenly
my mind became an unread novel.

frozen grapes
taste just like summer
even through the peachy springtime.

I asked you to cut me some slack
not my cherry garden
don't make me bleed.

Don't apologize
for your whore-moans.
Your body aches for womanhood

Croissants
are a French woman's best friend.

Life in the big city can get a bit hectic sometimes.
Have a bagel.

The thing you are most afraid of.
Write about that.

My lips are starving
from the hunger
of kissing yours.

You were in nature
amongst sunflowers
in the peaceful park side
But I am made of rivers
and in that way
I could have drowned you.

You create your own soundtrack
that's why we'll never live
in the same films

Smoking damages your lungs
replace tobacco ashes
with sunflowers
that way you'll live on forever

I can see your strawberries
you say it like it's a bad thing
why try and hide
what makes you

The woman that drives you
utterly insane
the woman that keeps you up at night
the one who'll inspire you
through the days
I want you to paint her.

the cancer stick between your lips
makes you dangerous

Perhaps I'm not searching for a man
perhaps I want a woman

What makes my strawberries different
from yours?
It's the leaves that are different
and you don't seem to mind
if I show those

My apple was poisonous
you should have known
before taking a bite

Even strippers have souls
their bruised peaches
are just a consequence
of your sick perversions

You'll worship Chanel in a man-suit
but a man in a dress and rouge
will still offend your religion

I braided daisies in my hair
let me live in Pachamama

What creates fear and discomfort in others?
Paint that.

Bad hair days
don't seem so bad
if you put yours up in a bun
after all
the hippies invented it

Roses aren't always red
especially when you choose
to violate mine

You'll wear all these masks
and yet you'll always play the same character
  we can all see right through you

You'll glance at beautiful women
in trains
little did you know
you could've looked for longer
through the reflected glass
of train doors.

- *Paris*

You were the perfect cup of English tea
but I prefer French coffee.

You'll first marry for love
then for money
but lastly out of bad habit

I don't dress for men
I dress for women
I prefer their fashion

We battle against our own minds
to determine what's real
who we are
what's life's purpose

Art is free.
But artists must conform
to certain norms.

I really liked her
so I asked for her lighter
I don't even smoke.

Why does my winged eyeliner
have to be perfect?
They're not twins, they're sisters

A minimal canvass
is but a movie screen
to project the mind's eye

Why respect one animal and hunt another
It was odd
the plants that nourished me
seemed to confuse you.

Giving birth to your art
is like watching your soul
escape your body

Do not mistaken my kindness for weakness
I am made of thunderstorms
and I will release them
when the sun's not shining

You'll watch the stars
with your best friend
and you'll see the galaxies, reflected
in their mesmerizing eyes
and think to yourself,
someone is going to seriously
fall in love with you
someday.

Tu me manqué
I don't miss you
You are missing from me.

When in doubt of what to wear
a black blazer
a white shirt
and blue jeans
is the French connection.

You said I was your earth
little did you know
I am made of galaxies

Who wants to fall in love with my mind?
Unbelievable
I have to do everything myself

They'll talk politics
with their lips
and erotica with their eyes

You don't need a companion
when you're drinking
I am the moon
I am the light
I am the toxic state
of your mind

You entered this life on your own
and you'll walk out of it alone
all the dancing in between
is only temporary

don't be upset if she turns you down

You're at war with what's natural
the leaves across our legs
would not grow
if they didn't want to live there

Art is about honesty
it's not always there to please others

You'll say you're angry
because you love me
now you wonder
why I love men
who act just like you

- to my step-father

Don't kill yourself yet.
Let's grab a whiskey first.

He'll pick all my daisies
and wonder
if I love him
or not

Take things slow
you're only seventeen
most people your age
don't even know what they want

Being told to give up my art
is like being forced
to use my right hand
when I was made
to use my left.

You create your own canvass
use your paintbrush
to write your own story.

I hope my son
looks like you someday
that way
parts of you can live inside me for months

Your husky voice
keeps me aching for days
it even makes me want to sing

Don't judge a tree by its leaves

when you haven't come anywhere close
to its roots.

How you see yourself

is how you allow others
to see you.

You wake up one morning
and notice a spot on your chin
don't be sensitive about
how you look
or it will be
the first thing people notice

Some people light candles
for their lost loved ones
I'll always light a cigarette

Injecting heroin
through my veins
could become my secret sexuality

You'll meet a man
with dark maroon eyes
and suddenly
brown eyes become your new favorite color

I am not a cave
for the prisoners of your mind
don't get yourself trapped
in cages
which don't belong to you

You'll travel through the Indian ocean
and set across footsteps
with the most mesmerizing woman
you've ever seen
she'll tell you her name
and suddenly you're almost certain
she's made you
feel things,
see things
that no other woman has ever
made you see
Do you see how limiting that can be?
She made you think
you'd never experience something
so tranquil, so exotic
a lust so bold and raw
ever again.

- Lust only consumes the mind, the flesh is temporary

Sure, you'll fall in love with
a woman
once, or maybe twice
but that's never the woman
you end up marrying.

You'll go through the motions
sadness will lead you to the pouring rain
and joy will seek you dancing over the moon
you never knew what grey was
you never did.

- For you, life will always be black and white

Don't mistaken my hungry kisses
for a starvation of erotic love
your gender just made things work
I wouldn't touch a woman for old money.

Have you seen Tamara De Lempicka's
women across her artwork?
The seductive, all-empowering
dynamic femme fatales
dressed in suits and
dressed in nude
with lips so soft
and eloquent voices, unheard
the ones that speak at the right time
I hope I raise my daughter to look
like that someday.

You undress yourself
and people are shocked
with your unconventional style
of clothing.

Sure, women can be strong
but there can be something so empowering
so unexplainable
about giving birth to a man.

I am made of rivers
pure enough
to cleanse away the pain
but if you don't worship my waves
I will drown you

You treat nudity like it's a crime
to be human

I stood naked before your eyes

but all you wanted to do
was hide

Don't undress me
with your fingers

I want you to explore my mind

Bastards will pretend
you're a bad person
to recover from the guilt
of what they've done to you

The thing about the movies
is that I'm unsure
if it's healthy for me to escape
in a world of wonder
and sweet violence
I can never tell
if films heal my pain
or destroy my reality

Don't waste any more time
loving all the women
who'd rather get hurt by men.

How could I expect a man
to love all the things
I hate about myself

Being gay is healthy
what's unhealthy
is living a life
where you try to convince yourself
that you're not.

Cross-dressing
doesn't make me any less
of a man
if anything
it helps me feel closer to women.

No one called Coco Chanel out
for dressing in a man-suit.
- *Let me be a man for once*

I don't love you with my heart
but with my mind
love shouldn't break you
it should make you grow
It is only natural
to feel pain
don't deny yourself
the chance to grow.

You are not with a man
and that's okay
you're ready to fall in love
with yourself first.

The oppression of either sex
eventually leads to the downfall
of the other

They say homosexuality is a choice
because they can't create lives
between two men
or two women

perhaps we don't want to procreate
who would wish on such a life
of pain and oppression?

I lay, waiting
for the kind of man who
[I'm not even sure]
 exists

Why do we associate
naked bodies
the purest form of human existence
with sex again?

Accept your mistakes
your flaws, your thorns
let your sunflowers grow
water them daily
sing to them everyday
tell them they're beautiful
help them blossom
let them grow
in your garden

You'll judge a man for choosing bananas
last time I checked
apples were the forbidden fruit

I am a woman
who sleeps with women
now I understand
what the whole hype
and obsession
with women's bodies
is all about

Don't apologize
for the mistakes
that helped you grow
    - *your leaves are made of experience*

You'll get repulsed
by the daisies on my legs
you'll tell me to pick them
I don't care if you love me, or not
you're just a gardener
who I never said was welcome
to step into my garden

It is only natural for a man
to grow his hair long
after all
he grows hair everywhere
as for the women
cut your hair short
that's how you like it everywhere else
anyway

I do wonder
if he plays with your golden locks
and holds you so close
the way I did before

I want to create films
which speak to others
in ways that I cannot

Maybe
I don't want to become your lost half
maybe
I am found
maybe
I am already whole

You'll judge a woman
for the stretch marks
on her creamy thighs
or the cellulite
that runs on her legs
for days
why do you think
she felt insecure
about shaving her legs
in the first place?

Why do we engage
in filtered conversation
to feel a sense of comfort?
Sometimes silence
can be the loudest roar

They way they stop speaking to you
says a lot of about their hidden
thoughts
the way they choose to escape
always remains
with you

My eyes are made of almonds
with strawberries on my chest
bananas for arms and legs
I wear my cauliflower curls
which protect my walnut brain
and yet you say
I need meat to survive?

- *Vegetarianism is only natural*

the wrinkles that dance
around your eyes
and those warm lips when you smile
creates a crimson fire
inside me

If the pain of unattainable love
never goes away
neither will the memories
flush away
    let them stay

These real eyes
will *realize*
your real lies

In a world of Tarantino's and Hitchcock's
be a Papados
fall in love with your own cinematic visions

My heart aches for his love

the ways my daisies
will ache for your spring

There will be women
who'll demonize you
they'll talk ash dirt
and they'll despise you
the most
to them
you must be a sunflower
be golden
and always shine

I was a Tarantino movie
but you were blind
and all you could hear
was the violence
and the thunderstorms
in my mind

You don't have to be
the rose among all the daisies
you just have to convince yourself
that you are

- how to be the most beautiful woman on mother earth

Don't judge a bruised peach
when you were the one
who disturbed all the fresh ones
from their mother trees

How does one
make peace with their body
when they're fighting
a civil war within
their minds

Your canvass
was not painted to impress others
your canvass is there
to please your own eyes
to excite your mind
it is there for you
to paint in color

You tore me open
like Adam's apple
the most forbidden
form of life
you forced me to speak words
I didn't know
created a language of their own

He tasted like sweet starvation
and I was sour hungry

My strawberries are not for you
to taste
they are there to nourish
my unborn son

You became a whore
with no self-respect or love
and now you wonder
why your son falls in love
with the idea of searching
for a woman like you

Listen, you're a lovely person
but I have a girlfriend
    - so do I

She was meant to be
the first woman
you ever loved
you're still searching
for her lost presence
everywhere you go
    - *Mother Earth, Pachamama*

No one appreciated
your unfiltered beauty
the temporary red marks
across your cheeks
made people scream

so you decided to put on a mask
that would last a *lifetime*

It's strange, isn't it?
Grown ups will ask
about the red spots across your face,
as if they've never gone through puberty before

- *fifteen*

You became a sunflower
in the hands of a man

who would not nourish your seeds

You'll hit your son
Every time he puts up a fight
he doesn't understand
wrong from right
he's only five
you teach him to mistaken
war with peace
which is terrifying
considering how he'll grow
to love women who'll shoot him
and trust women who'll harm him
just because
they begin to look
so much like his mother

I fucked her brains out, he says
but he doesn't know
what her walnut mind
tastes like

If I knew what loved looked like
I wouldn't let my daisies be picked
by men
who did not

A man
should never have
to get on his knees
and beg his whorish mother
for a love affair
    - *be a lady for your son*

He reaches for my mind
with his soft lips
and delicate fingers
it feels as if
he's scraping away
the rhino skin of a pineapple

when an actress begins to speak
during a filming scene
the director yells cut
and makes her shut up
this is how
women in this industry
have learned to live
with their legs spread open
like an empty canvass
with a mouth that is closed
because they're not allowed
to paint their own visions

we will grow through gardens
where our flowers are picked
by all the wrong people
to the point where
the right man may come along
he'll try and nourish your rose
without getting harmed by your thorns
after all
they're there to protect you
from harm

I could never tell
the difference between
someone being mesmerized
or shocked by my artwork
after all
these expressions look the same
to me

I shiver when you kiss me
I fear you're the pouring rain
and you'll destroy me

It was his cinematic lenses
which made me want to dance along
to the music
- *My life is a Tarantino soundtrack*

Change your lavender scent
trade it for something more masculine
make him think you found a secret lover

His words
make me want to explore
all the poetry
I wish I could write.

Stop asking women to smile
who says I want to smile
I don't want to curve my lips for you
I crave goddamn sadness

He asked me what I crave
what keeps me up at night
and takes me through the days
I told him I was a dancer

he asks me to perform for him
so I take of all my clothes
lean in closer to his ears
and whisper sweet erotica
I'll run my finger tips
through the back of his neck

I crave sunshine, I crave the light
his teeth begin to clench
his face will tighten
I make his pupils dilate
somehow,
I change their crystal color
I take a few steps back
and dress myself

I understand what you do, he says
you crave love
the kind your father never gave you
so you search for it in other men

You're watching me
as if you're filming me
capturing my movements forever
and this is how
you make a movie
out of me

Ever notice how
being denied an apple
makes you crave it
even more?

- *Why forbidden apples will always be my favorite fruit*

In Hollywood, every actress
was tall, thin and Aryan blonde
every actress posed like Monroe
every actress gave you the look
the look
of sex
the look
of power
in a world full of Shiksas and Aryan blondes

- I wish I was an actress

All of a sudden, your face
will be everywhere
on all the posters
in all the billboards
in all the movie screens
you take that moment
and you make sure
you turn it into your life

Acting, is not art
acting is prostitution
prostitution is sex
and sex means money.

- The world is sour poison
and you're the sweet addict

These films lack one thing.
Women's visions.
Your images, your frames,
the movements, rhythms and abrupt
shots of your films
they all deprive of that one thing.
Your films characterize the prisoners
of women's visions
of confined ideals.
In that way, it's still a rich man's world.

It's always a risk
to be in a long-distant relationship.
What if it doesn't work out?

Ah, but what if it does.

He carries narcotic temptations
and I, a vineyard heart.
Lust begins to drip
from my crimson lips
and he seems to enjoy it.

Conversation endurance is so important to me.
An intellectual connection is crucial
if you can't seduce my mind
don't expect me
to get
undressed

Why do I always have to drop hints
of myself in my artwork
and use that to explain myself to people?
I don't want people to see me
I want them to see you

- Maybe I'd like to share you with the world

Art is an expression of life
that transcends both time
and space
we must employ our souls
through paintings
to give a new form
a new identity
to the nature
of the world

It's interesting how you can tell
so much about a person
when they drink or smoke
who's doing it
for the thrill
and who's trying to
kill themselves

Introversion has directed me
my whole life,
everywhere
there's no escape

I never really cared about the money.
I mean sure, money
can buy you a great painting
it can transcend your visions into light
But goddamn, money
can't buy you a good wife

Wine 'gladdens the heart of man' [Psalms 104:15]
It is used to gladden and inspire us
at various times
it reveals a completed and perfect
human life.

- That's why I never finish my wine glass.

Sure, men will present nudity
in their films

with no core value

or artistic significance

but the language of cinema
will always have a pornographic influence

and that's where we turn Literature into life

You'll find parts of him
in every young man you meet
but in your eyes
no one could compare
to his mesmerizing touch
one man may have his sharp blue eyes
but when his hair is tangled
in your artistic lenses
you'll notice that each man
exercises his own freedoms
his own visions
one man may try to put a smile on your face
by bringing you your favorite cup of coffee
but you've grown so accustomed
to the way Dorian drank
you're left sipping on the toxic liquid
with a burdened
tar black heart

- Dorian Gray is my only muse

Some of us are naturally drawn
to each other
perhaps our atoms
were near each other
when the universe was formed
and over time
our atoms are finding their way
back home

Your mind

a beautiful servant
a dangerous master

Cinema

the blackest of all
human desires

- I was touched by God to make movies

At times
I forget to breathe
his writing transports me to a different place

- *Shakespeare*

Her luscious lips
are too precious for those cancer sticks.

- *Lauren Bacall*

I wake up to the sound of silence
there's something so comforting
in waking up
to the thought of you

Your redemption
will find you out.

I tremble at your visceral moans
these burning taste buds
make it hard to breathe
your cherry, but very wet lips
roll relentlessly across my tongue
this woman makes me feel
things that no man
could ever make me feel

- How I knew my best friend was gay

Young, virile and in love
I'm happy for you
I noticed you once or twice
it wasn't love, just fire
cold curiosity
I took a vow to celibacy
I am pure, I am clean
you were the end of all desires

Don't have sex.
You'll be the first to die
in a horror film

You're so caught up
in a world of transcendence
you can't even remember
what a woman's body
looks like
you
begin to crave
tentacle erotica

- *Why Japanese businessmen are repressed by Capitalism*

Nobody
ever falls in love with Cupid

- *I'm a Sagittarius*

His slender fingers
protected the curves of my breasts
your haunting lovemaking
cures my youth

I was bleeding womanhood
but nobody could see

- My first period

My peach aches
like a fresh leaf
of a shivering tree
my body quakes
at the sound of the waves
fantasies race
through my veins
like lightning

- *You must discover yourself first*

I'm sure you're a nice guy,
but I'm actually seeing someone

- silly bitch, I just asked for a lighter

My wife is on a diet
the first thing you lose
is your sense of humor

Coat your lips in burgundy.
It frightens people!

Don't nourish your demons
starve them out
with cancer sticks
'till they die

- *when I began taking drugs*

I'll never wear three-inch heels.
Why live halfway?

No, I can't bring you home.
My place has turned into a brothel.

- *why Greek catch-phrases will always be funnier than other languages*

Conversation, like erotica
should be intellectually stimulated
not intoxicated
with your artificial bullshit
and dry wine.

Don't mistaken her rosary
as a sign of dignity
that's where she snorts her cocaine from

- *Cruel Intentions*

I have a fear of putting on make-up
I wish I had the man-power

When promising to deliver
the Jews from Egyptian slavery,
God used four terms to describe
the redemption
I shall take you out
I shall rescue you
I shall redeem you
I shall bring you

FOUR CUPS OF WINE

The liquor on his lips
made me an alcoholic

She took the crimson apple
cut it in half
placed one of the two
between her legs
she spread them open
like a fruitful canvass
and asked me to paint her

call it sex, if you want to
but she turned it into art

- fruit never tastes the same
once you discover a woman's anatomy

At least with cancer sticks
you get to attend your own funeral.

Beauty trends will change
overtime
we will smile at mirrors
instead of iPhones

I braided sunflowers in my hair
so I could eat and breathe in spring

I'll always notice people's teeth
before anything else
somehow
adjusting your attention
towards a person's lips
makes them more beautiful
to stare at
It's also the closest thing
to their mind.

Where do I gain inspiration from?
You should know
I always dip my brush into my own soul
I paint myself onto my canvass
so my youth can live on forever

Her lips promised warmth
and touch
juicy nectar drips
from her peach
and it somehow sustains a form of life
yet unknown
to man
nectar that runs through our bones
and pumps through our hearts
lush, desirable
her peach betrays her
it aches to be touched, caressed
drawn to a state of ecstasy
relishing the pleasure of my fruit
for longer
just a little longer

Peaches
so juicy and sweet
dripping nectar on your fingertips
so messy to eat

Pomegranates
the fruit of the womb

Women
should not stop existing
the moment they give birth
to their children
Women
should embrace their new roles
as mothers
educate your children
show them the world
watch them grow
pass on your values
your culture
your philosophy
giving birth is like watching your heart
crawl outside of your body

Look at him
as if
you're gazing at the sunset

- How to make any man fall in love with you

Burgundy wine
begins to drip
between your lips
I think that's a sign that you've had enough to drink
look at you!
You're becoming an alcoholic

the woman you meet
in your bathroom mirror
should become your best friend
cherish her
and let her know she's beautiful
every morning

- I promise you better days

You'll give birth
to either one
of two men
a man
that wants to seek power
in the world
or a man
who wants to seek power
on a mattress

- it all depends on how you raise him

A wine glass
is always appropriate.

Never follow the rules of men
if you're a woman who wants to make history

There will be nights
where I'll watch the stars from my balcony
and think to myself
there must be millions
of women
sitting alone by their balconies
who dream about film-directing
I won't worry about them
I'm dreaming the hardest

- 12 am thoughts, City of London

radicals will revolutionize
with the love of Jesus
but the ones that are cunning
will win
with the redemption
of the devil

It's ironic isn't it
how the ultimate purpose of war
... is peace.

Old money
New money
money always talks
and I ought to listen

She's good from far
but far from good

Guess I'll have to become satisfied
with alcohol, books and vinyl records

You have terrible alcoholic breath.
You should cure it with books.

We need more Annie Hall's in this town.
More female suits.
More female ties.
Women that power-dress for the world
Women that are confident.
Let's create a style for women
who want to be the first female president.

There's something enticing
about going to prison.
You learn a lot of great dialogue.

- *Cinema imitates life*

Go for the boldest
most terrifying color
on the palette
in the case of movies
go with violence

Buy a painting
which makes you see
a million different paintings

Don't quit your acting job
because everyone told you to
do it because
you don't want to be
treated like a stripper
with lesser clothes
and a smaller brain

- Acting, and all the magic and the wonder that never comes along with it

He's very attractive
oh, for sure
But when he begins to speak
goddamn!
My brain gets angry

You have a secret lover
I should know about?

- *It should've been me*

Pachamama raises your consciousness
you become more human-
oriented
you're intensely dissatisfied
with the state of nature
modern political thinkers become so trivial.
You want to grab a modern politician
by his scruffy costume
drag him into the corners of space
and say
"Look at what you've done to Mama Pacha,
you lazy son of a cunt."

You always used to say
I wasn't like other women
how do you think that made me feel
being un-like other women
these are the mothers and sisters
which held me close
these are the women
I fought to become

- how I told him I was transgender

You can be the moon
bursting stars across the night sky

only if you want to be

you don't need to be
you don't need to let them drain

the ravishing rivers of your soul

You promised me you'd understand
and you promised that you'd accept me
for the man that I am
but you still call me, Mona
you know she died long, long ago
it makes me tremble and
it makes me shake
the sound of that name
you still see me as your daughter
even when my crimson face burns
at the sound of Mona
from all the times I've tried to scream
that I am now your son
why do you enjoy lying to yourself?
Do you think it sounds better?

Our gym teacher divided us into two groups
Boys on the left, girls on the right
as a non-binary individual
I just stood there
my gym teacher seemed confused
but he had it good
had I been bi-gender,
I'd be running side to side
back and forth
even worse
had I been gender fluid,
I'd be running in a circle,
screaming

These tears should never

be mistaken for weakness

they derive from your river soul
emanating freedom for comfort

and all of this

shall manifest

through the ocean in your eyes

Your eyes

were made from rivers

those dark blue waves were dancing
across the midnight sky

I wanted to sink in and swim
but I was made of fire

If he thinks your peach is bruised
because it has been touched
by many unwanted fingertips
just ask him
how many peaches has he bruised
perhaps
before he judges your bruised fruit
he should take a look
at his dirty hands

They had just met
and he started kissing her lips
at the back of the bar

- *Whatever, that's like a handshake in LA*

People from LA drink green juice
in the mornings
whilst New Yorkers tend to smoke cigarettes
followed after their first cup of coffee

- How Skinny Chic works

Music will expand your horizons
it flows through your branches
deflowering your soul
may it enrich
your interior rose

You'll lay in your sheets, shivering
to your sounds of imperfect silence
you'll ponder through the rivers in your wine glass
and run your dainty fingertips
around the rim
it's the only sound
which keeps your ears alive
and this is what it feels like
loneliness
the sound of glass, dancing
on its own
feels like your world is broken,
shattered
into willowed pieces
and all you want to do
is fly

Teach your son
he has to wait

- Raise him to be a gentle-man

If you have to stab it
to sickly death
cut it into grotesque pieces
boil it
skin it
fry it
beat it

- *You shouldn't eat it*

Learn to accept
the difference between
those who stay
to nourish your soil
from those who only ever come
to grab your fruits

- Go and make some lemonade with these sour lemons

I am losing parts of myself
which I refuse to reveal
in the same ways
which women keep losing
their virginities
unknowingly,
unquestionably
and almost everywhere

Have you ever been so close to death,
you can feel your soul
leaving your body?
Your heart stopping,
skin turning cold.
You become nothing
just a decaying human
wasting his breath.

You don't come back from that,
ever.

You rejecting my art
led to the manifestation of my paintbrush
falling in love
with all the canvasses
I've poured myself into

- thank you

She was an actress
and what does it feel like
to be an actress,
you may ask
it feels like the director's hand
grasping your throat
filtering your voice
with his artistic perversions
it feels like the director's hand
grasping your crimson mouth
and creamy thighs
some actresses might say
it's the sound of success
before the Oscar is earned
an artistic revolution
I say it's the sound
of masculine visions
grasping every inch
of your body
smoking away
the ashes of your soul

My hair is filled with wildfires
burning across the sand
red velvet flames
stream across my face
devouring radiance
through the crimson flows
of my mirrored soul

- Don't put my fire out with gasoline

Don't let the mimicking of birds
followed by the false voices of men
disturb the sweet nests
in your trees

- *Let Pachamama breathe*

I remember when I first got high
I dazed up at the sky, confused
and I could even see God
laughing back at me

You'll lay naked in bed
revealing it all
as he remains hidden
somewhere inside you
you're still searching for him
everywhere

- platonic relationships only exist in your mind

Mankind is cruel
Men are never kind

- *You belong to yourself first*

How foolish of you
to think that
you could've built a whole new life
inside your pomegranate womb

- My last abortion

The danger with art
is that I can never tell
if it's making me see
new, vibrant colors
or if it's making me
color-blind

The first thing they'll do is lead you in—
Always
to believing you need someone
to complete you for good
you fall into the habit
of love
thinking that having someone's body
wrapped around yours
will keep you safe at night
what a load of bullshit
most of the time
these partners in crime
are the ones
holding the knife

I tremble every time
he strokes my back
I fear he's stolen your knife

I'm not effortless
or a natural beauty
I'll paint my French fingertips
cover my ghostly complexion
with foundation and rose cheeks
apply my lashes with mascara
to make them look like they exist
I'll blow-dry my unwashed hair
and dress in monochrome.

- I sure as hell didn't get out of bed like this

He kisses his last cigarette
goodbye
and welcomes himself
to this new Nirvana life

- *Welcome to Pachamama*

When he walked out of my body
for the first time
parts of me died forever

- *giving birth to you*

They shot him right in the head
instead of shaking
I reached out for his skull

- Jackie

He inhales my crimson lust
with every inch
of his cocaine heart

I shiver
for the greatest minds
of this revolution
that will be destroyed
by utter madness

I'll be spending my nights
in her wild garden
branching the leaves
deflowering my baby

- *Karma ,*

Look at you,
you lost soul
you're still searching for my pomegranates
in every other woman

Maybe you haven't found her
because she's not searching
for you
maybe she's not even real
maybe,
just maybe
you're waiting for a he

You're life isn't cinema

happy endings

are just scripts

that aren't finished yet

I'm searching for a woman

who looks at danger
dead in the eyes

and gives me a wink

- I am searching for my future wife

Everything I eat is alive
to keep my body alive
nourish yourself
with pain, suffering and anger
and these emotions
will digest into your soul

- *Vegetarianism*

I crave a revolutionary lover
I want to feel the thunderstorm
cure someone's lack of insomnia
with endless conversations
at 4.4.3am
I want rage, I crave madness
someone you're willing to die for
who you also want to kill
someone that makes my blood shiver
that pulls my body closer
and makes sense of all my bones.

I'm really not your typical flower child
the whole drug scene is not for me
I am liberated
I am creative
and believe me
I don't need a silly buzz
to appreciate the sunshine
or the sunflowers in my hair

I take offense at that generalization.
Artists don't have to snort cocaine
from a stripper's hole
to turn money into light.

He was the summer tide, always
waving across the lives of those
who enjoyed vintage music
always out of place
unsure if he enjoyed the rhythms
of the band
or the wild waves
of the Malibu ocean.

Leo's golden waves danced
across the sunflower in the sky
surfing the cold waves
of the wild ocean
he pulls me along
the dirty sand

- At times, my son makes me forget I'm a woman

Because he's golden and
loves the wild(e)

- Why I named him Oscar

Your crispy mind
awakens
at the sound of dawn
the golden waves
across your face
lead you into space
it's a new morning,
sweet bliss
across your lips

it's now time
to breathe in,
    - *the sunlight*

He wore his hair golden, wild
with a spirit, so chaotic
he'll drag me into the midnight waves
a different kind of love, so erotic

- *Why all mothers are in love with their sons*

The first time
we spoke
the sun took a glimpse at his eyes
they sparkled into a cool shade of blue
I love eyes that do that
they appear so dark at first
then transform into a shade, so cool

- When blue eyes became my favorite

Sweet adolescent child,
you'll be a grown man soon.

- *whiskey and the talking cigar*

Don't water these leaves
if they don't nourish your trees

- You can shave if you want to

Light up
the fire in my loins

Do it again

Searching for a man
with a Lolita complex
doesn't seem so fun
when you're seventeen

He even asked me
if I ever read Lolita

Could you relax,
just a little?
Not every page
needs to be a masterpiece

- *give me some time, I'm working on my script*

I loved him. I really did.
It was amazing how he
immediately saw
my soft side
after weeks of speaking
how he told me I had a beautiful mind
how he didn't judge my skin or
the nipples across my shirt
as if my body causes great offence
and repulsion
to those
who cannot handle nature.

Liberty, Voltaire, New wave
Cinema.

You?

- *What keeps me up at night*

Why don't you act
in your spare time,
and get it out of your system?

- *when my father denied my art*

If I speak in the Elvish tongues of actors,
actors and directors,
but do not have their love,
I am nothing

- *Amorette*

You'll search for him
in every director you meet,
but in your eyes
no one could even compare to the pain.
Sure, one director may have
his sharp blue eyes, but when
his hair is tangled in your
cinematic lenses
you'll notice that each director exercises
his own freedoms,
his own visions.
One director may try to put a smile on your face
by bringing you your favorite cup of coffee
but you've grown accustomed to the way
your first director drank,
you're left sipping the toxic liquid
with a burdened,
tar black heart.

And you'll soon realize that
every director will have a flaw,
so miniature,
like his cigars
you come to realize
it's all in your head

- You have to become your own artist

We should preserve cinematic visions,
not culture.

It's about taking a 'thrill'
to a place where the people cannot
or will never go –
within the toxic minds of those
so beyond normality
where it becomes frightening,
but damn it, so compelling.

- The nature of Psychological Thrillers

One of the best lessons you can learn
in this life is to master
how to remain clam

- *Toxic Situations*

With every good film I see,
I feel reborn
(I feel alive)

I know Hollywood directors
don't really smoke.
That's why I've got this cigar at hand,
you're not supposed to inhale cigars
because then you'd still get cancer.
But take a look at me,
with this cigar at hand,
I look so magnificent,
like a Hollywood director.
I can't not smoke one!

- The Woody Allen imitator

It's not reality itself
that I detest,
but all the fantasies
of cinema
that don't come along with it.

Everyone said he was
a raving nymphomaniac,
that he suffered from
an insatiable, sexual appetite
but I got to know him
in ways which they didn't
and the truth was
he'd rather read a book

- The Sapiosexual

Men fell at her feet
she was larger than life
youthful and never aged
she somehow placed steel
in our backbones
she was holding up the entire country
and the whole world
with her breathy, flirty voice
she ran around with two presidents,
that's what they'll say about me
with that allusive charm
and enduring mystic
we were the stars
and she was the hurricane

- The first female president

He could have any woman that he wanted
he walked up to any one of them
and asked them
in ways which would earn
a slap in the face
for anyone who wasn't president

Marilyn always complained
that he was too hurried up
in his love-making

- The guy's running the country,
he doesn't have time for foreplay!

1. Most people are just looking for money, they will use you for it
2. You have to be shrewd with people to get what you want
3. Rich people have rich friends because they're the ones who understand them the most
4. Your relationship with your mother affects your relationship with everyone in this life
5. Your mother's relationship with your father influences your relationships with your partners
6. Not all family members will understand you, relationships should be a commitment on both sides and not just a blood connection
7. You control your inner peace, regardless of being surrounded by people who want to destroy you
8. You can have more than one soul mate, and one of the first soul mates that you'll have is your God-parent if not your mother
9. Never give up

- Things you'll learn when you're 18

How redeeming it is – but
also how tormenting – to be
an exception.

Get off my waves
you man-eating siren.

Oh my God
are you one of those
single-tear people?

- when sadness isn't madness, it is art

Real movies require
 the opening up of an actor
and at times
that can be painful.

- when I asked him to remove his mask

The real question is
do you control your brain
or does your brain
control
you?

I challenge you all, everyone
to look closer
the next time you go out
go to work
go to school
look closer
look at someone you see everyday
look past the normality of what you usually see
you may surprise yourself
as to what you truly do see
a strange kind of inner moment
when you realize that your heart breaks
for your worst living enemy
when you look past the exterior
and past the eyes
who are we really?
Do any of us truly know?

Life is not just
a span of time
set before us
all
it is a vast collection of moments
for us to use to the best of our abilities
and if we see the right way
if we allow ourselves to just,
look closer

- *American Beauty*

It's like
I'm on drugs
whenever I'm with you

They went to bed with Sugar Kane,
they woke up with me

- *Marilyn*

We're paying for the sins
we don't understand
because at one point,
we were taught that
it was simply human

- *nature*

You stabbed right through me
in the most brutal
way possible
to tear someone's wings
and force them to fly
a period in my life
where I was unsure
I could rise again

- in a strange way, what I mean to say is thank you

Your scripts
should never be based on
how many people enjoy them
your scripts
aren't meant to be pleasing
to the eyes of actors
and directors
your scripts
should invoke a darker impulse, a feeling
so nostalgic
your scripts
should frighten people's bones
and make their souls ache in pain
your scripts
should move people
back and forth
make them question
if they're faking their orgasm
or burning in hell

I want you to create a masterpiece
which allows me to enter
your veins
and reach
the deepest corners
of your mind

- Paint yourself to me

There's nothing more freeing
than undressing yourself to the sun
and pacing through the waves
of the ocean, freely

And when their words
make you feel pain,
just dive into the waves
let the ocean help you escape
drown your sorrows
and teach yourself how to swim

- *Today, I am free*

She carved an anchor
on the side of her ankle
it reminded her too much of the seven seas
her love for the ocean
a life she could never live
unless she let herself

- *drown*

You belong to yourself
before you give yourself
away
to
anyone
else

- in

I'm listening to our song
and it doesn't hurt me
like it used to

I enjoy uncomfortable silences,
but only with you

- Pulp Fiction

Most people's fruits are already bruised.
The difference between them and you is
they choose to not be honest about it.

- *Can you keep a secret?*

I never knew you could become sick
by loving someone too much

- *Take a Love Potion*

The worst thing of all
is when they all know your secrets
now you have none
left to excite yourself with

Parts of me escape
to each film I see
and then I die
each time
through the awakening
of human misery

I spend so much time
talking to people through cellphones
I think I've forgotten
what a human touch even feels like

It's okay for a man
to wear make-up
and paint his nails
to (un)dress himself
for the world
grow his hair out
and wear dreadlocks
if he chooses to

- *Who does the world really belong to, anyway?*

But how could you ask me to write
and recreate life
when I've already felt true pain
through the roots of my womb?

- Why female artists can't have children

You must choose
between me and your cigar

- when million dollar bills begin to talk

Men will leave their wives
and children
some will lose their lives
under the thunder caves
of sour violence
others will communicate through letters
for months, even years
and you complain
because he saw your text at 3am
and didn't respond
until 3.03am?

- why this society has it good and is yet so greedy

I am surrounded by women
who keep telling me to get married
it's a pity they don't understand
how I don't want to do this
in the same ways that
all these women
didn't want to get married
in the first place

- I suppose this is my way of protesting for my freedom, for my youth

I dreamt of my lover once
I was wearing his coat and his brogue shoes
in the same way all those young actresses you
see
wear female suits, inspired
by their director's clothes
directors will somehow form
each actress' identity
so no matter where the ladies would dance
across the lonesome noir towns
in all the cinematic worlds
their directors would always
be with them

The worst thing in the world
is to be wanted
by so many women
when all you really want
is men

You intertwine from just a handshake,
and, you complete every vein
and blood vessel
within

- how it feels to be touched by success

Open to the possibility
of a more vibrant
sensuality
enduring pleasure
and abundance
transformations are experienced
through the body
creativity flows
from your womb
to every root of your being

- The Sacral Chakra, your passion and pleasure center

I keep losing
parts of you
your mind
your pelvis
your heart
to other women

- You once told me I was your most exotic flower

I was sitting in my friend's local pub
when I saw her
she breezed in, so elegantly
just like she did
when I first saw her
I remember
I couldn't stop staring
back at her
tall, slim
sophisticated
the face of sweet Marilyn
wore her hair like Veronica Lake
along with the wardrobe
of Grace Kelly

- She was all the magic and the wonder in the world and I was curious

I wanted people to see
what real bravery was
instead of them
sticking to the belief
that bravery comes from a man
with a 45 gun at hand
ready to shoot
whoever disagrees
with his wild instincts

- Most people only judge you for it because they're afraid

You never meet lovers
you exist within each other
all along

Stop pleasing others
let this moment
in time
tear you open
and drain
all of the secrets
which hold you
back

You don't get in touch
with someone
by sleeping with them
you do it by healing
their crimson wounds
repairing the torn ashes
of their delicate skin

What women have yet to learn
is that no man can awaken
your secret sensuality

no one ever gives you

such power

you have to create it for yourself

I'll let you in on a little secret
holding grudges is mere poison
it will consume your toxic thoughts
within
we always assume that
anger is a gun
that attacks those
who harmed our souls
it's a lie
a double-edged sword
we only end up
harming ourselves

- keep yourself safe from harm

I'll lay in red-stained sheets
is it simply blood or is it my lipstick
you'll wonder
Do you ever reveal the raw wounds on your body?
Are they from my crimson lips? Or are they from hers?

They'll force feed you with pills
What about the thorns from your rose
are they still carved in your heart?
Have they become the nemesis
to your hubris?
And yet you continue
to wander in my garden
with no fears at heart
mistaking my roses for promises
and the sunshine for love
you continue
in failing to see the thorns
that are trapped in your heart
you still let them
force feed you with pills
to heal all these wounds

Didn't anybody ever tell you?
Wounds cannot be healed

they are nurtured with love
they are nurtured with art
they are nurtured by all those silent cries
you reveal to your dark soul at night

Your velveteen heart, it doesn't beat, hard
the way it used to
Your suspicious eyes, they don't recognise me
the way they used to
And your lips, oh, those lips
they never kiss, they never kiss me
the way they used to

- you never look at me the same anymore

I'll lay within your white sheets, almost nude, and I'll light up a cigarette. You'll stand there watching me, telling me how I finished drinking my coffee in a lightning. I told you it didn't matter because I wasn't tired or sleepy. You never laugh at my jokes, even though I know you appreciate them. Just a little. To be truthful, you never laugh at anything at all.

At times, I'll read novels whilst enjoying the sun in our balcony and you'll tease me for it. What are you reading all these books for, you'll ask. You'll discover the light of the world outside, in the real world, not amongst silly words kept in books. I'll grab you by the neck, push you onto the bed, forcing you to lay down and listen to me read De Beauvoir and Foucault. Do you know what literature is? Do you understand poetry, art, pain? Do you know, my darling, what pain is? No, you'll say, I don't know because I've never loved you.

- The world inside a bi-polar *schizophrenic*'s fragile mind

unfold the petals of your solar plexus
find the fire that burns inside you

- *chakra healing, it's the same with writing*

Men may have discovered the caves of fire

but it is women

who discovered how to play with it

About the author

Tina Papados was born on the 21st December 1996 in Athens, Greece. At the age of fifteen she moved to a sixth-form college in Cambridge, England. She is currently studying Politics at Queen Mary, University of London. Although she is currently an author and illustrator, Tina Papados is interested in a career in film-directing in the future.

Made in the USA
Columbia, SC
04 December 2017